Moolort Muses

Geoff Cobden

Copyright © Geoff Cobden 2018

First Published in 2018 by
Level Heading

All rights reserved. Without limiting the rights under copyright reserved above, no part of this publication may be reproduced, stored in or introduced into a retrieval system, or transmitted, in any form or by any means (electronic, mechanical, photocopying, recording or otherwise), without the prior written permission of the copyright owner.

ISBN: 978-0-6481726-4-2

Line drawings and cover pictures by the author.

Front Cover: Moolort grain silos and defunct railway siding.
Rear Cover: Bakers Swamp, Moolort.

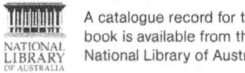

A catalogue record for this book is available from the National Library of Australia

Design and layout by Level Heading – levelheading.com

Level Heading

Author's note

If the reader smiles, sheds a tear or just plain nods the head, I'm satisfied ... After a thousand other obligations and pursuits that life throws up at one, I wonder where I got the time to compose and write poetry.

Considering the dozens I've torn up, burnt or censored, this offering is the cream of the crop.

I hope you enjoy them all, even those that may be considered "sour cream".

Moolort

People may ask, what or where is a Moolort? Moolort is a place in central Victoria, Australia.

No town, not even a store or service station. Just a place to pass through on the way to other destinations.

In the early years, when the first deep lead mining operations were in full swing, the area boasted three post offices and twenty-eight pubs.

The mining population must have numbered in the thousands, not to mention the resident pioneer farming settler families already established. At the time of this writing, the census population has dwindled to a meagre (but happy) thirty-two residents.

The Moolort Plains boasts a dozen or more seasonal red gum swamps that seem, these days, to be more dry than full. But when exceptional rain events occur they are transformed into water wonderlands and breeding havens for thousands of water birds, and resident raptors – eagles and hawks.

Surrounding these swamps are cleared volcanic rock paddocks that provide beautiful cropping and grazing lands, all overseen in the distant south by dozens of extinct volcanoes that circle from west to east in a calm but foreboding presence ...

The Pyrenees Highway which bisects all the above from west

to east was once one of the main thoroughfares for 1850's prospectors seeking their fortunes in the rich goldfields to the west – Maryborough, Talbot, Dunolly, St Arnaud, Avoca, at the base of the highway's namesake the Pyrenees Ranges – and a hundred other exceptionally gold-rich locations (see 'The Welcome Truth', page 60).

The Moolort Swamps provided a welcome stopover, with shelter, firewood, grazing for horses and game for the table, for weary travellers.

Now it's just a quiet pass-over point between towns where the ever present breeze caresses stands of wheat and canola, grapes, potatoes and other crops, and whistles through red gum foliage of century old trees that bore witness to Moolort's beginning.

It also inspires budding dreamers ...

Contents

Time	11	Relevant still	36
My Selection	12	Retreat	37
Where Else	13	Rap in Blue	39
Bagged	15	Spinner's Reward	40
Cowards of Bali	16	There's a Light	43
Deceit	17	Suckers	44
Despair	19	The Catch	45
Eddie's now a Senior	20	Awakening	47
Edie	22	Hoping	48
Eyeful	23	Chins up	49
Good old Days	24	The Question	50
Fine wine	26	The Gully	51
Destiny	27	Winding Down	54
Home sweet home	28	The Gift	56
Sorrow	29	My Wish	57
Humble pie	30	Warnie	58
Raindrops	32	Not forgot	59
Last Reflection	33	The Welcome Truth	60
Or have I?	35	It's a Furphy	64

Time

It flashed, it's gone, it disappeared,
It came it went, like wasted years,
Where have they gone? Those memories past,
I blinked, the days have slipped so fast.

They turned to months, the faces fade,
The crown of silk has slowly greyed,
They then transform the years of thought,
Of distant loves, and dreams cut short.

Those goals desired but not achieved,
Of webs that Father Time has weaved,
And how our journey's many trails,
Direct us to our holy grail.

What is it that we've so misplaced?
That left us with such speed and haste,
It has no rhythm or no rhyme,
What's gone? It's obvious, it's time.

My Selection

What would I select if I should, gain?
The poetry prize of olde Castlemaine,
What row would I pick in the bookshop's aisle?
That attracts my interest and makes me smile,

There's romance, adventure, science and history,
Or maybe a dose of fiction or mystery,
There are books for the learned, and books for the nerds,
And others that cater for all smiths of words.

So what do I seek should I have success?
My minds in a quandary, my thoughts are a mess,
I can't think of a title, no how, no way,
Well maybe ... "Fifty Shades of Grey".

Where Else

There's dawning in the bushland,
Of scarlet pink and blue,
Where bleeding skies turn amber,
And greet life on earth anew.

The shadows quickly shorten,
As the eastern ball ascends,
Whilst portly wombats shuffle,
To the safety of their dens.

Sounds of bushland then begin,
The sounds that reassure,
Magpies warbling from the heights,
Duck on swamp and moor.

The thumping of the wallaby,
Through scrub and gullies dense,
Or parrots cracking seedpods,
From their perch on tree or fence.

There's rivers with a majesty,
That wind throughout the land,
Or gurgle through a mountain pass,
With scenery wild and grand.

Where one might catch a fleeting glimpse,
Of lyrebirds in the valleys,
Or platypus floating on their backs,
Scratching furry underbellies.

There's colours of the spectrum,
To dazzle and delight,
Of red clay pans, lush green leaves,
And reef quartz, pink and white.

The brilliant showy splendour,
Of the rainbow parakeet,
Or the subtle yellow ochres,
Of a waving stand of wheat.

There's fragrance of a ferny glade,
Of bark and fallen trees,
Or that clean, fresh smell of rained on grass,
Carried on the breeze.

All these things and millions more,
Will greet you without failure,
'Where?' you ask. 'Where else, my friend.
'Australia, mate, Australia.'

Bagged

It glistened and shimmered in dawn's early light,
As the sun's golden rays devoured the night,
Darting and weaving, speeding up, slowing down,
It dived and it surfaced, attracting the brown.

He cast to the rises and worked the lure well,
And guided its progress where the big fishes dwell,
The lake was a mirror, the surface unbroken,
As rainbow and brown's feeding instinct was broken.

He witnessed a swirl and a splash at the take,
And a pink flash of silver shone through the wake,
The hook jaw rose upwards and leapt for the sky,
As the rainbow cartwheeled in attempt to deny.

But the angler persisted and kept the rod bent,
And let the line run till the quarry was spent,
Then the trophy was landed and proudly admired,
And given its freedom before it expired.

Cowards of Bali

It happened again on the holiday isle,
Wide-eyed innocence, wrongly defiled,
Bali bombers they called them, or a terrorist throng,
But to call them these names is as big a wrong.

To those who refer them, all Downers and Howards,
Call what they are, sick twisted low cowards,
From their leader's despatches of bravery are showered,
But the world knows what we know, their true name is coward.

There's no pride in achievement of winning a battle,
In killing a kid on a beach with a rattle,
If you don't like our culture, or don't like our face,
Settle it front-on like men, face to face.

We now understand why your actions are farce,
'Cause you know if you fronted, we'd kick your scared arse,
Forever these acts will unite the world's free,
And be known for all time as the cowards of Bali.

Deceit

[This poem was composed a good thirty-five years
prior to publishing]

We used to hide from Mum and Dad,
Before the knot was tied,
And we'd sneak off to St. Kilda,
Where our favourite fish was fried.

Necking on the foreshore,
Or the ti-tree down near Rye,
We'd excuse our late arrival,
With a shaky alibi.

"The car ran out of gas",
"Or the road was blocked again",
On a balmy summer's evening,
"We couldn't see for rain".

We'd have to ask our best friend,
If he'd seen the show at Hoyts,
So our alibi was concrete,
When asked of our exploits.

Her Dad would look upon the Merc,
Decidedly aloof,
And ask an explanation,
For the heel marks in the roof.

We'd bribe her little brother,
With a coin to buy some sweets,
And I'd make hot milk coffee,
Whilst she rearranged the sheets.

We thought that when we married,
We'd be free of all these lies,
We wouldn't have to hide again,
No more wheres and whys.'

But you wouldn't want to know it,
We wouldn't die for quids,
'Cause now we're pushing forty,
And we're hiding from the kids.

Despair

When you've exhausted all your patience,
And just about despaired,
When you've wrecked your car on rotten tracks,
A dozen flats repaired,

When your search for gold
Has cost you more than you have found,
And that dragging feel you feel,
Is your behind upon the ground.

When you're sure that Eveready
Owe their profit all to you,
And if you don't find something soon
Your wife is gunna sue.

Remember that the more you try,
The more you have a shot,
The chances are you'll win,
(But more than likely not)

Eddie's now a Senior

[Author's note: this next work was composed for a pommy mate from the Bowling Club. I think it explains itself.]

Val asked me if I'd write a verse,
In memory of Ed's past,
To celebrate this special time,
The years have slipped so fast.

It must have been a lean year,
That created Eddy Senior,
But it started with a swagger,
Cause the same produced Mick Jagger.

If I knew him any better,
Or shared his early times,
I'd write of all his exploits,
With anything that rhymes.

But I know not of his childhood,
His manhood or his teens,
I know not of his latter life,
Or any in-betweens.

Was he a famous author?
A soldier or a queen,
Were his leanings for Rock Hudson?
Did he dream of Norma Jean?

Was his temperament forgiving?
Did he rarely suffer fools?
Had he ever heard of "two up",
Or been to Aussie rules?

So I'm sorry if my verse is vague,
I wish not to be rude,
I'm afraid I'm like the rest of you,
I just came for the food ....

Edie

[Short for Grandma Edith]

There's a soft, waxen curl that falls on her brow,
She's striking, she's gorgeous even for now,
No makeup, no lipstick, its natural class,
They had no such things in hard times gone past.

Her eyes are so honest, open and clear,
Reflecting her heart, so kind and so dear,
The shape of her nose like a sculpture from Rome,
And a smile on her lips saying, "friends, welcome home".

High cheek bones and forehead, a proud perfect chin,
Thin eyebrows, soft earlobes, with beautiful skin,
There's a tear in my eye as I gaze at her face,
How I'd love to have known her to kiss and embrace.

But the photo of Grandma when she was so young,
Is all that remains, 'cept the memories of Mum.
You've been gone many years now, to heaven in shroud,
But dear Grandma if you're listening … "Jesus, I'm proud."

Eyeful

*[Much to my displeasure, and much to my family's great amusement,
this next event really happened.]*

The dog was just a pup, a playful little tyke,
A Weimeraner bitch you couldn't help but like,
She'd gambol in the veggie patch, and frolic on the lawn,
Inquisitive, mischievous, from dusk to nearly dawn.
She'd search for newfound mysteries, sampling every find,
She'd chew and taste and sniff and chase, to satisfy her mind.

'Twas on a Sunday morning, I'd let her out to scratch,
She circled round the backyard, then found the veggie patch,
I hadn't noticed anything, there hadn't been a sound,
Till I saw her making skid marks, her behind upon the ground.
"What's the matter little girl? I called her to my side,
Have you got worms? Are you ok? What's that in your backside?

It fluttered in the morning breeze, and drooped towards the ground,
A stocking used to tie the beans, to keep the veggies sound.
I grabbed it with a dextrous hand, she took off like a Bondi tram,
And with a yelp she reached the end,
the stocking stretched then gave a sigh,
And recoiled back into my eye.

Good old Days

You don't know till they're over, what "good old days" were,
Till you reminisce, look back, to some it's a blur,
To sit quietly and think of events of the past,
Smiling to oneself as memories come fast.

Of the iceman and baker with old horse-drawn carts,
The giggles of playmates, the open-air marts,
Of that tall kid next door who called you a prick,
And the look on his face when you picked up the brick.

When the pickets on fences were all the same shade,
When everything purchased was once Aussie made,
Of me old mate "Stick" Parker, and the day that I cried,
When told of his passing, eighteen and he died.

Of Mum and the flat iron, the ice chest and safe,
Newspaper in the dunny, oh how it could chafe,
Dumplings, and yabbies cooked in the copper,
And a hot water bottle with the loose fitting stopper.

Of a sixpenny haircut, a deener of chips,
Our Saturday pilgrimage to the afternoon flicks,
No modern contraptions, the heat waves intense,
Relief was obtained with a wet hessian fence.

Those times when marooned on the road with a flat,
When strangers would stop and throw in his hat,
No comforts we had, the like of today,
It was harder with some things, but a lot simpler way.

In one hundred years when people talk of better ways,
They'll reminisce their bygone times,
As the ones they recall,
As the "Good Old Days".

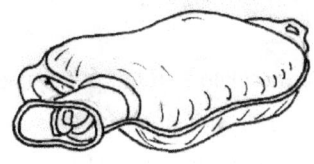

Fine wine

It was one of those moments that held me transfixed,
At the sight and the sound of the falls,
I was awe-struck and glazed as I stood in the mist,
I even stopped scratching my balls.

As the water cascaded in foaming white pools,
And the spray gathered thick on my glasses,
We gingerly stepped across green mossy rocks,
And collectively slipped on our arses.

I knelt at the swirl and cupped a cool drink,
And gulped down sweet nature's fine wine,
But the dream was destroyed as I glanced up the pool,
And witnessed a stream of urine ....

Destiny

I can hear her gentle intake,
As she stirs me in her rest,
She knows not that I listen,
To the heaving of her breast.

What comfort through the night,
As I see her sleeping face,
And touch with gentle fingertips,
Caress with fond embrace.

The warmth her skin delivers,
Gives my restless sleep content,
And I realise in reflection,
What her partnership has meant.

Our lives we've spent together,
Lovers, partners, mates,
Our love will last forever,
Our destiny awaits ....

Home sweet home

[This was read out on ABC radio by Ian "Macca on a Sunday" in a segment called "Why I live where I live".]

Hey, Macca, we've heard all the stories,
Why all the folk live where they do,
Of beautiful landscapes and rivers,
Blue Mountains, the Reef, Kakadu.

With concrete and brick and neighbours that stink,
There's no redeeming factor,
Our spot has pollution, syringes and drugs,
Resembling a nuclear reactor.

We can't sleep on Sundays,
What with yapping of pets,
Then there's leaf blowers and Victas,
And overhead jets.

No blue wrens for us,
There's nothing more finer,
Than watching a native,
Chased off by a mynah. [Indian that is]

So why do we stay here, why stay in this hole?
If we're so disenchanted and bored,
It's simple, dear Macca,
This place we call home, is all we can bloody afford.

Sorrow

She was just a country girl,
Reared upon a farm,
Loving and devoted,
A fly she wouldn't harm.

The first time that our paths crossed,
She was on a bed of straw,
Our eyes met in that instant,
And I think I loved her more.

Her brother was a bully,
Her sister raised the roof,
And her parents watched in silence,
Looking decidedly aloof.

They introduced me to her,
And we clicked like old friends do,
And we grew to know each other,
Our year's together true.

Its twelve years now, this love affair,
My sorrows I can't drown,
Cause the Vet has just advised me,
We have to put her down.

Humble pie

They said he couldn't do it,
When he headed for the hills
That miners and prospectors,
Were a pack of dreaming dills.

The words "you couldn't do it",
Had echoed round his head,
It urged him on whilst digging,
And haunted him in bed.

"A waste of time and money",
Was the cry with scorn and mirth,
"You're a loser", said the doubtful,
"And you have been since your birth."

So he learned and studied hard,
And researched to drop the odds,
He'd show those smirking sceptics,
On return with rolls of wads.

And here he was returning,
After weeks of sweat and toil,
Thinking of those words,
That had made him dig the soil.

His wife had nagged and pleaded,
"You know my dear you shouldn't",
They said he couldn't do it,
And he proved them right ... he couldn't.

Raindrops

Listen to the raindrops, hear them teem,
Watch them cascade, fill that stream,
Rivers of life that swirl and curl,
Washing the leaves, glistening on burl.

See the rise on cracked dry banks,
Drown the sound of echoing tanks,
Galvanised iron beating in rhyme,
Cleaning the gutters, washing the grime.

Those claps of thunder and cracks of light,
That shook the ground with nature's might,
The dog's gone hiding in awestruck fear,
The dust has gone the air is clear.

So listen to the raindrops, hear them teem,
Witness the landscape turning green,
See the mushrooms break their seams,
As shafts of sunlight radiate beams.

So thank the heavens and kiss the wife,
And watch in awe the newborn life,
Lie back in bed and wistfully dream,
Listen to the raindrops, hear them teem.

Last Reflection

[This was another one read out on radio by Macca. What Macca didn't know was that it was inspired by an old bloke that Alex Pike and I met while camped at Murrin Murrin, east of Leonora W.A. Alex became a friend after wandering into camp many years earlier and was amazed that we not only showed him our nuggets but invited him to camp with us and share the experience. We would coordinate our prospecting trips to coincide with his.

Macca always spoke kindly of Alex, having interviewed him on an earlier show. During one of those trips we met a wizened old bloke who described his years as a kid on the diggings. We were later to hear that he had been found dead beside one of the dry creek beds.]

Rusted cans and white clay pipes,
Bottles glistening in the early light,
Decayed remains of the old oil lamp,
That lit the camp in the dead calm night.

There's a bent horseshoe near a stump cut clean,
The boiler dormant that once made steam,
Sun-dried bricks where the scrub now grows,
Breakaway slopes contoured dry blows,

A whisk of breeze stirs long dead embers,
The same warm breeze the old man remembers,
Seventy years had come and past,
When as a lad he felt the blast.

He reminisced of the green rock moss,
Of starry nights and the Southern Cross,
Of the old horse Nell, dusty and brown,
And the heartbreak endured when she was put down.

There by the creek, ever dry, full of sand,
Sandalwood trees and a Salmon gum stand,
Were the blows that he'd worked as a lad twelve years old,
And there by the creek he'd found his first gold.

Tears welled deep in tired old eyes,
As he thought of the crows and the dingo cries,
The flapping of canvas, the scrape of the shovel,
The piling of quartz, separation of rubble.

The thump of the stamp, and call of the mail,
Bore water clear and lapping the pail,
Aroma of damper, and grinding of grain,
Fragrance of flowers and sweet smell of rain.

Yes to others this ruin would seem just a mine,
But old men who dream regard it a shrine,
Each relic of interest, each rusty old can,
That litters the landscape, has a story, a plan.

He gazed one more time at the memories of youth,
Excused his return with reflections of truth,
As the breeze rustled leaves he thought of his bride,
And lay by the creek and peacefully died.

Or have I?

Where is the inspiration to compose another verse?
Sitting here just musing my thoughts are getting worse,
I've creased my brow, doodled words, reminisced and more,
I've twiddled thumbs, researched books, even paced the floor.

But can I conjure up a rhyme to satisfy my thirst,
No blooming way, what's wrong with me? Am I about to burst?
But wait, I think it's coming, a marriage that will rhyme,
A sentence that will balance and beat an even time.

They said I couldn't match this word,
The balance wouldn't hinge,
But "eureka" I have found it,
I've rhymed it with "orange" ….

Relevant still

Remember the screen days of milk and honey,
When actors had class and comedians were funny,
Of Tracy and Bogart and Lauren Bacall,
The African Queen, and flicks that enthral.

The Wizard of Oz, and Citizen Kane,
Gone With the Wind, or Singing in the Rain,
Casablanca and City Lights, North by Northwest, It's a Wonderful Life.

Three stooges, Bud Abbott and Lou Costello,
Dean Martin and Jerry, oh, how we did bellow,
Of Laurel and Hardy, Jack Benny and Hope,
Who delivered their lines without need of soap.

And did we not marvel at the screen's silent king,
The first to thrill millions, the master ... Chaplin,
They amused us, they thrilled us and filled us with mirth,
The stars of the past who witnessed the birth.

A hundred years have flickered by,
yet still they make the grade,
Their class defies the years, their acting will not fade,
And in a hundred years from now, the critics will declare,
The skills our predecessors had were just beyond compare.

Retreat

'Tis man's domain the only place
His ego rules the roost,
It welcomes him to ease the mind,
And gives his pride a boost.

A slightly soiled leather chair,
Beside a stand of wicker,
Upon which sits his tools of trade,
The trusty T.V. flicker.

A large flat screen adorns the wall,
His window to the world,
A patriot flag hangs proudly near,
Its corners torn and curled.

A table of the coffee type,
Resides upon the floor,
Its legs upon a woollen rug,
Not quite Christian Dior.

The wall behind, a photo
Of his favourite football team,
The series numbered for the few,
That wish to hold the dream.

And so with beer in hand he rests,
In his cosy safe retreat,
His legs upon the footrest,
His dog content asleep ....

Rap in Blue

There I was in dreamland,
Fast asleep and counting sheep,
Exhausted from a hard day's toil,
Retired in slumber deep.

I thought it but a dream,
When a far off distant sound,
Wrestled my unconscious,
To the objects all around.

The chorus that awoke me,
Was the beauty and the trill,
Of a gorgeous Aussie blue wren,
Serenading from the sill.

His gentle tapping on the glass,
And sweet melodious tune,
Displayed his plumage electric blue,
The hen birds all but swoon.

I slipped the sheets and slowly,
Aroused myself from slumber,
And slammed the bloody window,
To shut out his noisy number.

Spinner's Reward

[This is a true story which occurred in the Loddon River below the Macorna channel at Dingwall, near Kerang. The man involved was my friend Lenny Ross, returned serviceman, hunter and fisherman. RIP Lenny.]

He'd learnt to fish when just a youth,
And loved it with a lust,
He'd fished for fun and just for sport,
And once to earn a crust.

It wasn't that the man was tight,
Or keen to save a quid,
It's just he hated waste,
And losing spinners blew his lid.

He'd strolled a hundred streams,
From the Murray to the Yarra,
Catching rainbows, cod and yellas
By the bagful, and the barra.

The thought of losing spinners,
Was to him like spilling wine,
He'd strip off to his birthday suit,
And follow down the line.

One afternoon in April,
With the river running fast,
He got snagged a proper beauty,
And he'd only had one cast.

So, with certain parts quite frozen,
And a face resembling blue,
He undertook the rescue,
With a vengeance seen by few.

The line ran round an old gum branch,
And through a patch of weed,
And snagged upon the object,
That had done the dirty deed.

The spinner wouldn't shift,
But the object might, with force.
So he heaved with all his might,
And nature took its course.

Struggling to the surface,
Gasping air and feeling sick,
His eyes befell the culprit,
And his tongue began to lick.

In his arms he clutched a roll of wire,
Barbed and rusty brown,
And a hundred glistening spinners,
Like a coronation crown.

They dangled there in clusters,
A dozen at a time,
The accumulated losses,
Plus a mile of tangled line.

It took a morning's work,
To retrieve the lures attached,
A labour most rewarding,
Though his hands and arms were scratched.

So pleased was he with all his luck,
He gave his thigh a whack,
And feeling not the slightest guilt,
He threw the object back.

There's a Light

*[A course of chemo and radiation
for Lymphoma inspired this work.]*

You'll get through it they say with conviction,
It's a breeze is their hollow prediction,
You're tough, you can take it, we're sure you can make it,
It's only temporary infliction.

But my defences have gone on the blink,
I'm just not as tough as they think,
My hair's fallen out, I've developed the gout,
And my taste buds have gone down the sink.

But I'm not giving up, I'm holding top cards,
I've got all you lot at my back,
There's family and friends, and even a nurse,
And waiting for hire, a bloke with a hearse,
[He's one I'll be giving the sack]

Five months of chemo, my bodies turned white,
My temperatures gone through the roof Fahrenheit,
I'm over the worst, radiation to come,
Five zapping weeks will see it all done,
But the best news of all that thrills with delight,
I'm near through the tunnel ... and I see a light.

*[Five years have passed and those that know have pronounced that
I am in remission – a nice way of saying 'on standby'.
So far so good.]*

Suckers

"Do you fancy a peanut", the old lady said,
As she offered the jar with a nod of her head,
"Old Bill just don't like em," she continued to state.
"They clog up his bowels, and get stuck in his plate."

We'd been painting the kitchen for the old dear for free,
In return we'd accepted biscuits and tea,
"Just help yourselves, boys. You empty the jar,"
She said with a smile, adjusting her bra.

So we emptied the jar scoffing nuts by the score,
If she offered again we'd no doubt have had more,
She returned after tea and cleaned up like new,
And uttered the statement that turned us both blue.

"I see you've enjoyed them, I hate to see waste,
That useless old rotter just ain't got no taste.
His gums can't chew peanuts, he just likes to lick.
All the chocolate around them, he sucks till he's sick.

The Catch

'Tis nature's dawning seen by few,
With verdant pastures tipped with dew,
Shadows lengthen then return,
Purple haze from ripe lucerne.

Rabbits scurry, foxes stalk,
Bronzewing pigeons dodge the hawk,
Insects swarm above the lake,
As trout and natives feed the take.

The angler casts with expert ease,
And flicks his fly into the breeze,
The swirls of feeding fish draw near,
His heart is thumping in his ear.

The take is clean, the line is taut,
The reel screams out, the trout is caught,
Be careful, don't be heavy-handed,
The fish is nowhere near yet landed.

Take it easy, let it run,
It's huge, its fight not nearly done,
It leaps and cartwheels in the drink,
Its glistening flanks shine silver pink.

But then a white flash plummets past.
His jawline drops, he's all aghast.
The trophy fish which was a winner,
Is now a Sea Eagle's favourite dinner.

Awakening

God gave me a gift and I just didn't know,
I've felt all my days that I've nothing to show,
There have always been clothes, abundance of food,
Family and friend to pick up my mood.

There's been fresh air and wildlife and clear mountain streams,
And freedom from guilt and low self-esteem,
I've mostly had work, and kept up the rent,
Though most of my dough I seem to have spent.

Why me, with the puncture, why me, breaking tools,
Why not me, the bloke that just won the pools?
With envy I've cursed and even blasphemed,
Please, let me win was the vision I dreamed.

But then I woke up and it hit like a truck,
I already had fortune, I didn't need luck,
It's been there beside me for all of my life,
My soul mate, my lover, my beautiful wife.

Hoping

Here I sit despaired and broke,
Knowing if I fail I'll croak,
The future's bleak, but so's the past,
I've got to find a nugget ... fast.

The tax man's been, the rates are due,
My nose is running, I've got the flu,
The car needs tyres, the brakes are low,
The paintwork's chipped and lost its glow.

The muffler fell off down the track,
And the tent burnt down by the time I got back,
I got stung robbing bees of their nectar,
And backed the car over the metal detector.

So I'm back in the diggings again at last,
Trying my best to forget the past,
There's gold nearby, well so's the rumour,
Thank Christ I've still got my sense of humour.

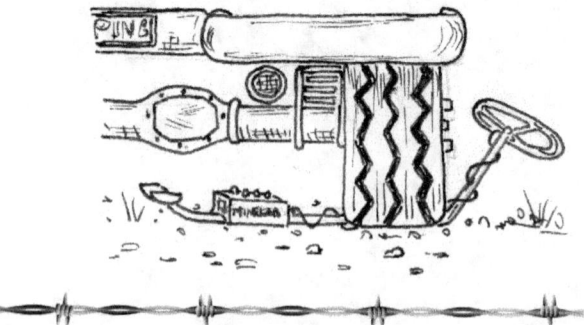

Chins up

[This was sent as a card to be hung on the Christmas tree in the foyer of Melbourne's Peter MacCallum Cancer Centre.]

Don't give up hope
And please don't despair,
It's scary I know
But you'll get back your hair.

Your strength will return,
With the help of the staff.
You'll enjoy life again,
Be happy and laugh.

I know 'cause I've had it,
And now in remission,
And guess what?
This summer I'm going fishin' ...

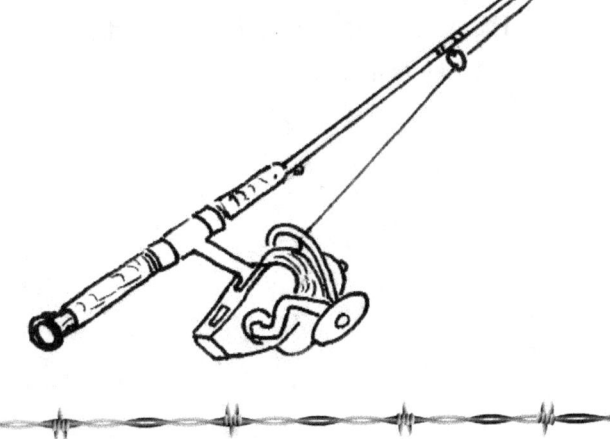

The Question

Over fifty years I toiled a trade,
Learnt the ropes to make the grade,
Scaling ladders, digging ditches,
Solving problems, correcting glitches,
I've wielded brushes hammers and axes,
And fifty years I've paid my taxes.

And now I'm retired I'd like to mention,
That trying to live on the old age pension,
Gives older folk a heap of strife,
Be it sole survivor or man and wife,
'Cause the future's filled with apprehension.

When a leader can stuff up the country for years,
Leaving welfare and pensioners with nothing but fears,
Then raise their own salary and treat us like jerks,
Retire on five mill, not to mention the perks,
The question to ask, to debate and discuss,
Was their contribution really worth fifty of us?

The Gully

Let's try and paint a picture of a scene
From years gone by,
Of a gully in the goldfields,
Where the bush was hot and dry.

As far as one could see were men,
Stout-hearted, working there,
All in the same pursuit, in hope,
An answer to a prayer.

Approaching from afar,
A sound so deafening and weird,
Would greet the weary traveller,
Enough to curl his beard.

The sound of rocking cradles,
At least a thousand fold,
Would echo round the ranges,
In their mad pursuit of gold.

As we wander through the gully
And gaze from left to right,
A kaleidoscope of nations,
Creates a wondrous sight.

There's Chinese on the hill up there,
And Germans on their right,
And working yonder cradle,
A Swede with all his might.

There's old and young, fair and dark,
All toiling for their share,
And keeping rein on all these folk,
The trooper on his mare.

A little up the gully,
And over to the east,
Tents are pegged,
And pots on fires,
Cook the evening feast.

"Feast", we say, well meal, if that,
Good food and water's rare,
Why just to buy one egg,
Would cost a trip to Melbourne fare.

A hundred pounds a ton for flour,
And spuds are threepence each,
And as for fruit, a pennyweight of gold,
For just one tiny peach.

The commissioner's camp is on the crest,
Buying for the crown,
And nuggets fill the strongbox,
To go to Melbourne town.

Troopers tending horses,
Traders selling wares,
The soil is rich, and reward is there,
For any man who cares.

A century has passed now,
But all this comes alive,
To all us weary dreamers,
Who finally derive.

That if there was a time machine,
And if we were so bold,
We'd join our predecessors,
In the gully with the gold.

Winding Down

I've tramped the bush from Cape to Tassie,
Played football, cricket, and run in the gift,
I've fought in 'Nam, and shot wild ham,
And watched the sands of the Gibson shift.

I've prospected on the Western quartz,
And felt the surge of Northern heat,
Fished the Murray and Darling branches,
And stared at the stars in a stand of wheat.

But now I'm confined to a single room,
With a bed and chair and not much more,
And it takes forever to shuffle out,
To the dining room through the corridor.

The nurses are nice and the food's not bad,
But most of the company's sick and sad,
We all know our time is near,
When our kinfolk visit us less each year.

Even though my prime is done,
My thoughts are those of twenty-one,
I dream of my youth and the love of my life,
Who spent all those years with me as my wife.

She's gone from me now,
And I'm lonely and scared,
But I know she'll be waiting,
To greet me ahead.

Yes, we're old and winding down,
And our life is all but through,
But just remember, that there,
But for the grace of God … goes you.

The Gift

She's a mother, they cried, she's got special powers,
She's a mother, they echoed, give her some flowers,
What gift has the Lord empowered with love?
That makes her so special, a gift from above.

What special ability, makes her so rare?
What natural gift does she flaunt with a flare?
Her skills are recorded, since puberty came,
She's a woman, a girl, a sheila a dame.

This gift that she's blessed with,
She'll take to her tomb,
Her gender distinguished,
Because of a womb.

My Wish

I wouldn't hold her hand,
When Mum pampered and harassed,
I'd wrench my arm away,
Feeling coy and all embarrassed.

I figured I was big-time,
Too cool to be adored,
If she would show affection,
I'd yawn and say, I'm bored.

She'd steal a kiss in public,
In front of friends and mates,
And I'd recoil in horror,
With complications it creates.

I'd dart my eyes from left to right,
And quickly peck her cheek,
And hope no friends had seen the deed,
And think of me as meek.

But now I'm old and Mum has gone,
I'd show it on T.V.
I'd hug and kiss to show my love,
For all the world to see.

Warnie

The wickets came with magic spun,
And once he nearly made a ton,
His stamina and belly fire,
Was fuelled with "gotta win" desire,
His strength was built, or so it seems,
With cans of Aussie-made baked beans.

If it wasn't for his indiscretions,
Double dates and all night sessions,
Retirement that his fans thought early,
Punched above his weight with Hurley,
Who flew the coop with sapphire band,
"That bloody thing cost sixty grand."

We had our doubts before the spider,
But that became the big decider,
He proved himself and held his nerve,
Faced his demons without reserve,
If Shane had not been such a lad,
He'd have been the best skipper we <u>never</u> had.

Not forgot

[This short stanza was penned after another school shooting In USA.]

We know them not but still we weep,
Taken to their Lord to keep,
Their journey's end like wheat stalks reaped,
A shocking waste that cuts so deep.

These beautiful lives, needlessly taken,
Not forgot and not forsaken,
We stand in stunned disbelief,
We mourn your loss and share your grief …

The Welcome Truth

*[The true story of the finding of the World's largest gold nugget,
as gleaned from historical facts.]*

Two Cornishmen from Tresco,
an island off Land's End,
Had heard of gold in Aussie
and decided to attend.

The big man was John Deason,
his mate was Richard Oates,
They arrived in early 'fifty-four,
and spent eight years prospecting,
According to my notes.

Feeling the pinch by 'sixty-two,
they gathered up their tools,
And travelled to Moliagul
through bush and scrub and pools.

The western slope of Bulldog,
was the gully they selected,
And worked the ground nine inches deep
with a puddler, horse connected.

They toiled for seven years,
up there amongst the sticks,
Although they found the odd grubstake,
[one went thirty-six].

John Deason pointed out to Oates,
the familiar dark red clay,
Below the Black Reef outcrop,
going downhill near halfway.

"I'd like to try that site", said he,
"where those diggers pitched their tent.
I reckon it's gold bearing."
And so started the event.

'Twas Friday fifth of February
in the year of 'sixty-nine,
When they came upon the "Welcome"
on that wonderful incline.

Too hard to lift, he broke a pick,
and decided that they'd wait,
Till dark set in and all was quiet,
he'd work with Oates, his mate.

They removed the golden prize that night,
and hid it in their hut,
And sweated out the weekend,
keeping doors and windows shut.

They circulated word
to all the friends they trusted,
Of a party on the Monday eve.
More than half the town they mustered.

The find lay on the table,
covered well from prying eyes,
The shades were drawn, the night was dark,
the bush was checked for spies.

And John Deason, with a flair,
disrobed the sleeping giant,
And watched his friends' reaction,
to the golden mount defiant.

The largest piece of gold,
the world had ever seen,
Was resting on that table.
Even wealthy men went green.

Two and a half thousand ounces
transformed the group, awestruck
They stood in silent wonder,
disbelieving Oates and Deason's luck.

To both the lifelong friends
it was a saviour in a manger,
And from that night the world would know
the nugget "Welcome Stranger".

Note: This nugget, the largest ever recorded in the world, grossed 2,520 ounces. When cleaned the actual net weight resulted in an astonishing 2284 ounces 16 pennyweight 22 grains (about 68 kilograms). And they didn't get it all. Around 110 years later, a friend of mine located and dug out a nugget weighing 1.5 ounces from a spot not 50 yards away from the monument erected on the site of the discovery, using a metal detector.

It's a Furphy

What the furf's a Furphy,
Have you ever heard the word?
I asked my old mate Murphy,
The name seems quite absurd.

And Murph replied, "of course it's real,
It's been a tool of trade,
They've used it for a hundred years,
They're also Aussie made."

'Twas in the 1880s,
When John Furphy Built a tank,
For stock and farming folk alike,
From it their fill they drank.

The horse-drawn tank of cast and steel,
Saw service in the war,
And quenched the thirst of Diggers,
From the Somme to Bullecourt.

The drivers of the carts were known,
To stretch the truth with rumours,
And a new word, "Furphy", was conceived,
By sceptic dry consumers.

www.ingramcontent.com/pod-product-compliance
Lightning Source LLC
Chambersburg PA
CBHW072108290426
44110CB00014B/1869